To my mom, Jan. Thank you for allowing me to be your dream girl. What an honor and privilege it is to be your daughter.

To 007, here's to twenty more years of seizing the day every day with you by my side.

To my Dad, Brady, here's to our mutual love of books and quotations.

To the dreamers, believers, and those seeking to seize the day—may you be inspired.

TABLE OF

SEIZE YOUR LIFE:

HOW TO CARPE DIEM EVERY DAY

Jasmine Brett Stringer

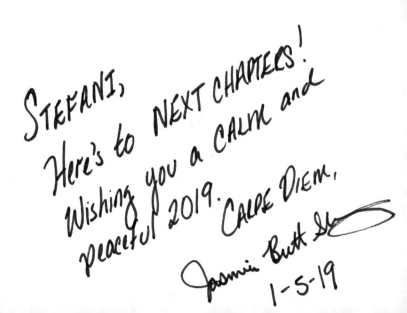

STEFANI,
Here's to NEXT CHAPTERS!
Wishing you a CALM and
peaceful 2019. CARPE DIEM,
Jasmine Brett St
1-5-19

ISBN: 978-1-63489-018-2
eISBN: 978-1-63489-024-3

Library of Congress Catalog Number: 2015959361
Printed in the United States of America
First Printing: 2015
20   19   18   17   16   5   4   3   2   1

Cover Design by Nupoor Gordon
Interior Design by Kim Morehead

Wise Ink Creative Publishing
837 Glenwood Ave.
Minneapolis, MN 55405
www.wiseinkpub.com

To order, visit www.carpediemwithjasmine.com or call 1-800-901-3480.
Reseller discounts available.

SEIZE
YOUR LIFE

HOW TO CARPE DIEM EVERY DAY

Jasmine Brett Stringer

WISE
Ink
CREATIVE + PUBLISHING
2012

CONTENTS

PREFACE

I've used the phrase *carpe diem* since studying Horace's famous odes in high school. As I've sojourned through life, Carpe Diem has shifted from a phrase that I enjoyed saying to a way of life, because I have a deep understanding that:

- Life is extremely short.
- Life can positively or negatively change in the blink of an eye.
- This moment, this day, is all we really have.

Often when people hear the words *seize your life* or *seize the day*, they think that they have to do something grand, adventurous, and exotic—or that there is a monetary cost associated with it. I contend that we all have the ability to seize our lives and Carpe Diem every day through awareness, action, and appreciation. This book is filled with personal stories and learnings from my quest to *Carpe Diem Every Day*. It is my desire and intention that this book will inspire and empower readers to seize their lives and, with the actionable guidance found in the book, will create a conscious shift of people striving to *Carpe Diem Every Day*.

INTRODUCTION

During the summer of 2015, I made a friend named Ms. Bea, who I met at a hotel in Ixtapa, Mexico. She was confidently speaking fluent Spanish to other guests, unabashedly animated, and wearing a stunning, bright coral blouse. Not long after I noticed her confidence, she sauntered over and asked me about myself. The conversation we had changed my life.

At ninety-eight, she was a retired scientist who worked until she was eighty at the New York Academy of Sciences. An avid traveler, she had chased solar eclipses throughout the years, explored rivers and railways across the world, and spent her summers studying at Oxford University. She'd visited every continent and more than eighty-five countries. I was in awe of her willingness to travel alone. Her two children and husband had all preceded her in death. Her daughter's death was more recent, and she shared with me how, at the age of ninety-three, losing her sixty-five-year-old child had been especially difficult, but she had still chosen to keep going, to continue living.

The more we chatted, the more inspired I became by her passion and zeal for her life. With her one-hundredth birthday not too far away, not only does she have her next trip planned;

she has her next several trips planned. "Live your life on your terms," she said to me at the end of our first conversation. We've since had many more.

> Not only be present, but also embrace each moment—even the tough ones—with intention.

Ms. Bea is an example of someone who has decided to seize her life. To not only be present, but also to embrace each moment—even the tough ones—with intention. *We are often so consumed with planning our lives that we forget to live our lives.* And let's face it: many of us complicate our lives with procrastination, hesitation, and fear. I believe that Carpe Diem-ing, or Seizing the Day, begins with the decision to seize the moment. How do we do that? We miss an infinite number of moments that simply slide by each day. Ever notice how quickly moments become days, days become years, and years become decades? We have a choice, at any time, to recognize the distinctness of our moments—even the dull ones.

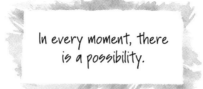

In every moment, there is a possibility.

Most people think Carpe Diem is about grandiose experiences, buying expensive toys, or taking fabulous vacations. It isn't. To seize your life means deciding to live in the present and to make the most of every day. After all, tomorrow is not promised. Your adventure is happening right in front of you. When you live Carpe Diem, you stand firmly in the adventure of today while remaining empowered for the Divine fortune you know awaits you tomorrow.

This book will share my principles on how to expect, attract, and receive all that life yearns to offer you. That's right: a Carpe Diem mindset doesn't believe in earned blessings that are beyond your reach if you aren't perfect or if you've suffered severely in your past. A Carpe Diem mindset accepts that the Universe is seeking, longing for, and designing your best. You cannot seize abundance if you carry fear or regret in your heart. Missed opportunities and mediocrity are only a few hurdles standing between you and the gift of Carpe Diem. By the end of this book, I believe that you'll be ready not only to live authentically but also to seize all that your heart desires.

CHAPTER 1

Believe, Trust, and Have Faith

You get in life what you have the courage to ask for.
—Oprah Winfrey

Oprah, my self-proclaimed aunt, is someone I had always wanted to meet. I admire her tenacity, and, growing up, I watched her show every day. Once I declared that I would meet Oprah, I actually journaled what I might ask her, not *if*, but *when*, I met her. I believed that, one day, my dream would come true. In 2002, I visited the Oprah show for the first time and was one of those fans who hung on the railing to shake her hand as she made her way to the stage. I'll never forget it because it was a show where Oprah was raising money for nonprofits. The show was powerful, and it left the audience in tears, and I was more inspired than ever. I knew in my heart that I would see her again someday.

Ten years later, after I was laid off from a corporate sales job, I found myself in a state of uncertainty, but I was ready to create the next chapter of my life. On a whim, after connecting with Oprah on social media and admiring her from afar, I requested tickets for one of her Lifeclass shows. I thought I was dreaming when, at the close of the show, Oprah asked, "Where's Carpe Diem? Where's Jasmine?" I nearly fell out of my chair. Was Oprah referring to me? I raised my arms and frantically screamed, "I'm here!" and Oprah responded, "I'll see you backstage."

Did Oprah just invite me backstage? Yes, she did. I had an instant sense that the Universe had gifted me an opportunity to know without a doubt that my intention was heard. I met Oprah backstage a few minutes later. We embraced as if we were friends who hadn't seen each other in ages. This moment was not only a dream but also a *want* come true. I was nervous, but I had always known this moment would come and that I would be speaking to Oprah one-on-one.

Two months after that meeting with Oprah, I had the opportunity to meet up with her for lunch. We have since connected several more times, and she recently gifted me a copy of her book, *What I Know For Sure*, with this inscription: *Jasmine, carpe diem indeed. Blessings in your life. Thank you for your unwavering support and being a carrier of the light.* For me, my relationship with Oprah was symbolic of something deeper.

> Remember:
> if you want something,
> there's no harm in declaring
> that you want it.

There is power in *want*. What are some of the things you would love to see happen in your life? I love the line from Paulo Coelho's *Alchemist*, "And, when you want something, all the Universe conspires in helping you to achieve it." Remember: if you desire something, there's no harm in declaring it. In fact, the real harm is in not acknowledging what you want in the first place. You might be asking yourself, "What if I don't get what I want?" or "I know what I want—but is it reasonable?" Without faith, an intention or desire doesn't have a chance. Not only is your faith powerful; it also pours fuel into what has already been promised to you. Oprah is a remarkable soul whom I was destined to meet. Sure, life throws us surprises. Often, however, *we're the ones in our way.*

> When you want something,
> relentlessly desire it without
> apology or fear, especially if it
> aligns with your purpose and
> propels you forward.

Believe, Trust, and Have Faith

- Reflect regularly on your goals and how you can bring them to fruition.

- Connect with your inner child— the *you* that you were before pragmatism told you what was safe to want. What were those desires?

- Make a list of five specific things that you want to happen in the next thirty days. Revisit your list regularly, and add to it. Put a checkmark next to *intentions* as they become *realities*.

REFLECTIONS ON HOW I WILL

Believe, Trust, and Have Faith

CHAPTER 2
Be Prepared

Ask for what you want, and be prepared to get it.
—Maya Angelou

Seizing opportunities as they present themselves requires preparation. And not the intense overthinking and obsessive planning that make many of us feel like we are drowning. *Preparation is simply being ready.*

Before your next opportunity comes knocking, be ready to sprint through the door with all the tools and resources ready to make the opportunity not only possible but also affirming.

During my freshman year, out of the blue I was invited to travel to Europe with the president of my college and his wife. It was an opportunity to trace the steps of John Wesley, the eighteenth-century theologian responsible for the creation of the Methodist church. Our university president happened to know that I was a practicing Methodist, and so I suddenly had a tremendous opportunity placed in my path. In this instance, being prepared simply meant having a passport, which I had because I knew that travel was important to me.

I've met so many people who have put traveling at the top of their bucket lists but don't have a passport—which, by the way, is a phenomenon I've observed mostly in the United States. I can tell you from experience that you never know when a cheap ticket may show up to take you to one of your dream destinations.

You've probably brushed up against a marvelous opportunity simply by being at the right place at the right time, right? Well, I don't believe moments like those happen by accident. When an extra concert ticket suddenly becomes available, or you're placed in first class after purchasing a coach ticket (real story), or an offer for the perfect job position falls in your lap—this is evidence of how the Universe wants to offer you the best that life has to offer. However, it'll be more rewarding for you if, when an opportunity presents itself, you're already positioned to receive it. The power of Carpe Diem is the expectation that good things will always come your way. Be prepared when they do.

Time and chance happen
to us all, and the key is being
prepared when your time and
chance comes.

Be Prepared

- Ask yourself, "Am I prepared for the surprises, gifts, and opportunities that come my way?"

- Make a list of what you need to become more prepared for your dreams to come true (i.e., if you want to travel internationally, get a passport; if you want a new job, update your résumé; if you have dreams of starting a business, create a business plan).

- Reflect on how well prepared you were the last time an opportunity came your way. What might you do differently next time?

REFLECTIONS ON HOW I WILL
Be Prepared

CHAPTER 3
Fully Engage

You need to let the little things that would ordinarily bore you suddenly thrill you.
—Andy Warhol

My mom used to tell me, "Whenever you do something, do it right." For some of us, "good enough" is merely getting it done. Think about it: how many times throughout your day are you juggling multiple tasks and are so intent on completing all of them that you're jumping from one thing to the next and simply going through the motions? In reality, it's not practical to be one-hundred-percent engrossed in everything required of us, but when I really started to think about it, I realized there were more things I should be fully engaged with—things I simply wasn't giving ample attention. For instance, I noticed that at dinner parties, I was prone to check my phone for emails that I felt needed an instant response instead of enjoying an outing with a friend. I often allowed my mind to wander, contemplating the next appointment on my calendar and how to make it there on time. I realized that seizing my life meant releasing myself from the pressure of maximum productivity, especially if I couldn't be fully engaged while being productive.

Now, I make a point to fully engage wherever I am. If I'm at the airport, it's not unusual to board a plane with several new friends that I've made while waiting because I've decided to enjoy myself. I view conversations with strangers as a way to engage throughout my day.

Make a point to uncover the beauty often found beneath the surface of stories and the details shared with you.

Make a point to uncover the beauty often found beneath the surface of stories and the details shared with you.

BE IN THE MOMENT AT YOUR JOB

What would it feel like to fully participate in whatever you're doing, wherever you are in your life, even if the circumstance is temporary? For example, a woman I'll call Sheila was offered a new job as an assistant manager and was told that she would be promoted to manager the following year. Sheila decided that, since her new position was temporary, she'd put a limit on how much she was willing to do. After all, she knew that she was management material, and her promotion was right around the corner. While she did an outstanding job performing the duties of an assistant manager—she was pleasant to work with, and she completed all the tasks asked of her—she was never quite as engaged as she could be. When invited by other assistant managers to activities outside of work, she saw it as a waste of her time. After all, she'd planned to be an assistant manager for only a year. Why should she bond with folks she wouldn't be working with permanently? Sheila fell into a common trap. By not building a relationship with those colleagues, she missed the opportunity to get the most from her present circumstance. She focused so much on her next job position, which actually took longer than a year to materialize, that she missed what her current position had to offer.

Think about it: are there opportunities in your current circumstance that you're missing because you're too focused on what's happening next?

BE IN THE MOMENT WITH YOUR FAMILY AND FRIENDS

There are plenty of reasons why we don't fully engage, and we all do it. Our relationship with technology is perhaps the biggest reason we fail to be in the moment with our family and friends. We live in an age where we are constantly connected through electronics, and at times, our electronic connections take priority over our human-to-human connections and prevent us from truly engaging with our friends and family. Television is no longer the only electronic vying for our attention. Now we have to contend with individual pursuits like email, text messages, social media, videos games, music, and the never-ending pulls of work. These things are all easily accessible and find a way to keep us from being in the moment with our family and friends. Most American families are starved for true quality time in which family members are fully engaged.

I've also heard countless stories about children whose families move frequently and how, after a while, these children don't even try to make friends or connect with the community because they know they'll be moving again.

It's normal to try to anticipate what's going to happen next, but seizing your life means deciding to dedicate yourself to where you are right now.

Fully engaging allows us to connect and build relationships with those around us and also within our community. Connection to others is a primal human desire, and we can't fully engage if we're constantly connected electronically or if we're unable to enjoy our present life.

CARPE DIEM GUIDELINES TO

Fully Engage

- Assess the areas where you know you aren't fully engaged. Decide where you need to take action and where you need to let it go.

- Make a point each day to focus on one of the areas where you need to take action, and fully devote your attention to that specific area; for example, a conversation with a friend, preparing dinner, or spending time with a loved one doing his or her favorite activity.

- The next time you notice yourself becoming preoccupied with the future, stop and remind yourself of what's happening in the moment and why you're grateful for the present moment.

REFLECTIONS ON HOW I WILL

Fully Engage

CHAPTER 4
Seek Authentic Connections

Connection is the energy that is created between people when they feel seen, heard, and valued—when they can give and receive without judgment.
—Brené Brown

I live in Minneapolis, a city with a reputation for being challenging for transplants like myself to make long-term friendships with the natives. Many Minnesotans remain close with their childhood friends, and they don't always put emphasis on creating new friendships. I'm not a shy person, and I enjoy making new friends, but when I moved to Minneapolis, I had to put forth more effort to make connections than I had in any other city.

I learned a lot in the process. Before, I hadn't paid much attention to how I connected with people and places. Now, charged with constantly being proactive, I was really beginning to take note of how and why my interactions occurred; it was fascinating to see all the new opportunities that those intentional connections created. You can't choose your family, but you can choose your friends, and I found that if you put in genuine effort, you can choose some great ones and they really do make the world a better place.

STORIES BIND US

Perhaps it's because I'm an only child, an extrovert, and the daughter of "older parents," but I get a major thrill out of making new connections; it's definitely one of the ways I Carpe Diem throughout my day. But over the years, I have had to come to terms with the fact that I'm not good at remembering names. I'd cringe when someone I'd met previously would recognize me and call me by name but I wouldn't know his. After some time, I realized that, while I might not be good at remembering names, I always remembered stories.

Stories are where you can find your connection to a person and even to a new destination.

So whenever I would get overwhelmed with the idea of having to create new friendships or bond with a new place, I would instead focus on going on a treasure hunt for stories. I've met most of my friends by way of exchanging stories. I believe that our stories truly do bind us, and our connection is born from a mutual understanding that we're all in this together. My introverted friends would find that putting in the genuine effort to create authentic connections is an essential part of their lives. They might not enjoy large parties, blind dates, or networking events, but they enjoy the spontaneity of a walk around the lake on a brisk fall evening as well as the right opportunity to share their story over a cup of chamomile tea.

HOW AUTHENTIC CONNECTIONS HAPPEN

Unfortunately, when trying to build relationships both personal and professional, we often miss the mark because we overcomplicate the process. We think connections come from dinner invitations, coffee dates, and joint outings that either lead to yet a deeper connection—or fizzle out entirely. In reality, the most authentic connections happen in reverse. After establishing common ground (most often through sharing stories) and going deep in the beginning, the bonding over a meal or coffee happens organically. In this scenario, we're not "courting" a friend to figure out if we want him or her in our lives. No, we're deciding at the first story swap that we share a connection so that our interactions thereafter are about learning and growing together. It can be scary.

There's risk in peeling back the layers of your soul and baring it before strangers. We all remember the feeling of being the last kid chosen for the kickball team or having a close friend compromise our trust. Seizing your life is a blast when you have friends who are also seizing their lives.

- Are you surrounded by friends who know you intimately and who call you out when you're not being authentic?
- Are you consciously surrounding yourself with people and experiences that add dimension, perspective, and insight to your life?

The opportunity for authentic connections in your life lies in your willingness to be vulnerable and to openly share your experiences—even the ones you hold close to the chest. Within friendship lies one of life's ultimate gifts.

Seek Authentic Connections

- Contemplate whether you over-complicate the process of making new connections.

- Make the commitment to offer a personal story in your first conversation with a new connection.

- Pick one day a month to follow up with important connections existing in your life.

- Visit one place that you haven't yet seen in your city or town. Journal the experience, and reflect on what you loved most about it.

REFLECTIONS ON HOW I WILL

Seek Authentic Connections

CHAPTER 5
Allow for Flexibility, and Embrace Change

The only way to make sense out of change is to plunge into it, move with it, and join the dance.
—*Alan W. Watts*

Plans change, people change, expectations change, and routines change, and often, our pain comes from our inability to be flexible through change. This can be very difficult, since change is the only certainty in the world today, and the frequency with which things change increases daily. It seems that the more things change, the more we're tempted to keep things the same—the familiarity of our comfort zones is a tough animal to fight. And yet truly seizing your life requires openness and more—rolling with the punches to get the most life has to offer. Have you ever noticed how you can't get to the next exhilarating chapter of your life without letting go of the current one?

> To truly seize your life, you must be open to rolling with the punches; that's how you get the most that life has to offer.

My mother modeled the importance of allowing for flexibility and embracing change. Growing up, it was my responsibility to write our annual friends-and-family letter, and I often found myself writing, "My mom has reinvented herself again and is now doing something entirely different." Throughout my childhood, my mom enjoyed careers as a flight attendant, a real estate agent, public school teacher, business consultant, and, most recently, an entrepreneur. Her ability to reinvent herself professionally as needed through the years due to corporate restructuring, as well as the evolution of her interests or our family's needs, taught me to embrace change.

> Being flexible and comfortable with change provides peace in the present moment.

I know that it's uncomfortable to throw caution to the wind, and that's why we start with the little things. Add intentional, routine-changing practices to your every day. Instead of driving to work the same way, take another route. Instead of leaning on your comfortable evening activities, shake things up on purpose. Order something different from your favorite restaurant next time. Resist the urge to settle into a "norm" that doesn't challenge, stimulate, or provide joy in your day to day.

Try this: Add intentional routine-changing practices to your every day.

Allow for Flexibility and Embrace Change

- Ask yourself, "Is flexibility tough for me? And if so, why?"

- Do one thing this week that is completely outside of your routine.

- Journal a recent instance when being flexible positively impacted an outcome, even though it felt uncomfortable.

Allow for Flexibility and Embrace Change

CHAPTER 6
Forgive, Free, and Release Yourself from the Past

I've come to trust not that events will always unfold exactly as I want, but that I will be fine either way. The challenges we face in life are always lessons that serve our soul's growth.
—*Marianne Williamson*

One recent Sunday morning, I was lying in bed, listening to the white noise blaring from my television as I read a collection of journal entries from people around the world. I was captivated, reading personal stories of tribulation and triumph, when it occurred to me that each of the lives I was becoming immersed in was like so many people in the world (myself included). At one point, these tremendous change-makers were part of the Walking Wounded—those we often think of as having been physically injured in a battle or major accident but are still able to walk. However, I think most of us fall into the second definition of the Walking Wounded—those who are suffering from an emotional wound.

The Walking Wounded stride among us as real-time reflections of past disappointments, mistakes, and failed relationships—the hiccups of life that hang us out to dry. Yes, the Walking Wounded have a special way of communicating as pain seeps through their pores and an air of sadness drapes over their words. When you're one of the Walking Wounded, pain from the past is immortalized in the present, and it drives every thought; this pain hijacks possibilities and holds dreams hostage. If you're lucky enough to have any motivation at all, you'll likely be asking the question of all questions: Why me?

However, there's no simple answer to this question. And nothing good comes from asking, "Why me?" Yet it's easier said than done to resist the urge to ask it. I've made that mistake myself, and when you do, it opens the door to self-pity, bitterness, or worse, self-loathing. The best things you can do are practice forgiveness and release yourself and others from the baggage that you're carrying. Our wounds don't have to paralyze us. When they do, we can't live productive lives and create and maintain healthy relationships to get the most life has to offer. Like physical wounds, emotional wounds heal with time, but they also often leave a scar on our hearts, reminding us of the wound.

Practice forgiveness, and release yourself and others from the baggage that you're carrying.

As someone who has struggled with forgiveness and releasing myself from emotional turmoil, leaving the Walking Wounded club is a process. It doesn't happen quickly, nor is it easy, which is why many of us prefer to stay in the wounded space, especially when we have friends and family who have decided to also pitch a tent there. It's work to move yourself forward, and there will be moments you meander backwards, depending on the depth of your pain.

But, there's no greater reward than seizing your life from the trenches of an emotional setback. Here are the steps:

1. Acknowledge that something wrong has happened.
2. Take time to first reflect, and then decide how you want to think about your setback.
3. Control the message of your pain before it becomes etched in your soul.
4. Finally, develop healthy steps to protect yourself.

> Protecting yourself means
> establishing healthy boundaries
> and also strengthening your
> support system.

Now, as a Carpe Diem enthusiast, I want to make it clear that I'm not advocating that you protect yourself from future pain. First, it's impossible to do this, and also, I'm a believer that pain serves a purpose. Protecting yourself means establishing healthy boundaries and strengthening your support system. It's also important to note that it takes time to process pain. Your ultimate goal should be to make sure that you don't allow your pain to become a crutch.

When you immortalize pain, you feed resentment, the desire to pursue revenge, and all-around self-destruction.

I choose to believe that our experiences shape and form our lives into beautiful pictures, like the tile, glass, and stone that make up mosaics. They form an artful masterpiece of lessons, revelations, and awakenings. Suffering also offers opportunity, which in some sense does mean that everything happens for a reason. We need all of our experiences, both the wonderful and trying, to complete our pictures, because they shape who we become. I've decided to embrace all my wounds and scars without allowing them to paralyze me.

So my questions to you are:

- How do you handle your wounds and the scars they leave?
- Have you left the land of the Walking Wounded?
- Do you know where you are in processing your pain?

Our experiences, both the wonderful and trying, complete our personal masterpieces because they shape who we become.

Forgive, Free, and Release Yourself from the Past

• If you're emotionally wounded, don't ask, "Why me?" Instead ask, "What can I learn from this experience?"

• Make a list of the people and experiences from your past—those that are keeping you from appreciating the present. Release yourself from their hold through 1) meditation or prayer, 2) a fortified support system of people who encourage you, and 3) a commitment to not allow emotional trials to keep you stuck.

• When negative or defeating thoughts and memories, as well as toxic people, enter your space, seize your peace with unrelenting fervor.

Remember you have only one life, and you can choose where and with whom to invest your energy and focus.

Forgive, Free, and Release Myself from the Past

CHAPTER 7
Focus on the One You're With

See the light in others, and treat them as if that's all you see.
—*Dr. Wayne Dyer*

Unfortunately, there's a constant battle between how you use your time and the people that are demanding a slice of it. Then the inevitable happens. When we do spend time with our loved ones, colleagues, and clients, we aren't present when we should be. I don't know how many times I've heard former colleagues and friends regretfully speak about not really being "there" during their child's sporting events, practices, and parties because of work, social media distractions, or our other favorite external factors. We're in a constant state of distraction, or—let's be honest—we have self-focused obsessiveness, which often means the person across from us at the dinner table isn't getting our full attention. Whether you're thinking about your next appointment or dominating the conversation with updates about you, it's quite possible that every person you spoke to today needed to *not only know* you were listening, but also *needed to hear* encouragement or a compliment.

Maynard Jackson, the first African-American mayor of my home city, Atlanta, Georgia, had this endearing way of connecting with each individual he encountered. Despite being extremely busy running the City of Atlanta, he made everyone whom he interacted with feel special—no matter the venue or the barrage of folks vying for his attention. It wasn't unusual to see lines of people waiting to speak to Mayor Jackson or shake his hand. Yet when he spoke to you, he made you feel like you were the only one in the room.

We may not all have Mayor Jackson's charisma, but I know from experience when I'm giving my full attention in an interaction, it's more fulfilling for both the other person and me. I challenge you to take your next interaction with someone a step further and see it as an opportunity to plant something positive into the person with whom you're speaking. As we Carpe Diem in our everyday moments, we should pause when we're in someone's company to make sure we're giving our maximum focus, appreciation, and selflessness. I believe what we give to the one we're with comes back tenfold.

Focus on the One You're With

- Take time to nurture your important relationships.

- Next time you're doing an activity with friends, turn off your cellphone. Not hearing a ding signaling new emails, texts, or messages from apps will help your attention stay on what you're doing.

- Better yet, leave your cellphone in the car.

Focus on the One
I'm With

CHAPTER 8
Allow Yourself to Feel

Feelings come and go like clouds in a windy sky.
—Thich Nhat Hanh

Our feelings are the lifeblood of our day-to-day moments. They set the tone for the day ahead. If you're feeling energized, you'll accomplish more. If you're feeling fatigued, your day will reflect your fatigue. I believe in allowing myself to feel whatever it is that I'm feeling in the moment, which I admit at times can create an internal contradiction. As a firm believer in the power of controlling thoughts, I also think we should call a spade a spade and allow ourselves to feel our emotions. The key is to acknowledge feelings without allowing them to take center stage.

Remember the last time you felt incredibly overwhelmed? Maybe your inner positive voice said, "Be thankful," but at the same time, you heard another inner voice scream, "Something has to give!" Seizing the day means acknowledging all of your feelings—not only the ones that feel good. When I've noticed a feeling that I didn't like, it's often led me to "difficult" conversations, both internally and with others. I notice every feeling and allow it to show me something I might need to learn from or adjust. By allowing ourselves to feel and sit with all of our emotions, we become more complete. As Barbara Brown Taylor so poignantly writes in *Learning to Walk in the Dark*, "I have learned things in the dark that I could never have learned in the light, things that have saved my life over and over again, so that there is really only one logical conclusion. I need darkness as much as I need light." We need to feel all of our emotions and feelings because they enable us to be the truest form of ourselves, and they aid in fostering honest connections and allow us to authentically seize the day as opposed to distancing and numbing ourselves.

WHEN STRONG FEELINGS APPEAR

One of the most important questions to ask when you have a strong feeling is, "Is my feeling truth, or is it a fleeting thought?" I allow myself to feel what I feel, but I recognize that my feeling is just that; it's only a feeling. Because I feel unattractive on a particular day doesn't mean that I am unattractive. I like to view my feelings as data that indicate what I should pay attention to or reflect on further. If I'm feeling tired, I allow myself to feel it, and then I reflect on why I'm tired and what I need to do to feel less tired. On the flip side, if I'm feeling ecstatic, I allow myself to completely revel in that feeling.

> Allow your feelings to indicate
> what you should pay attention
> to or reflect on further.

Don't block your feelings. Blocking or denying your feelings won't work. There's a reason you feel the way you do. Feelings are often the gateway for your spirit to tell you something you need to hear and then pay attention to. I'm not suggesting that every feeling should force an action or reaction. Before you decide to act based on a feeling, I recommend simply paying attention to it first. Sometimes the acknowledgment is enough.

Allow Yourself to Feel

- The next time you feel compelled to block a feeling, don't. Instead, open yourself up to it and ponder what the feeling is trying to tell you.

- Reflect on a particular feeling you often try to suppress and why you do that. Journal the possible reasons you block the feeling and how allowing the feeling might help you.

- Notice your feelings more regularly, paying particular attention to how responsive or unresponsive you are to them.

REFLECTIONS ON HOW I WILL

Allow Myself to Feel

CHAPTER 9
Allow Yourself to Be

*These past thirty days, I have spent many of my
moments lost in that void.*

*And I know that many future moments will be
consumed by the vast emptiness as well.*

But when I can, I want to choose life and meaning.
—Sheryl Sandberg

Sheryl Sandberg, COO of Facebook and author of *Lean In:
Women, Work, and the Will to Lead*, lost her husband suddenly while on a family vacation in 2015. In keeping with the
Jewish tradition, she kept Shiva and Shloshim—the thirty-day
period of less-intense mourning that marks the completion of
religious mourning. After her family's Shloshim, she chose to
share her gratitude. She posted a raw, honest, and poignant
post for the world to see on Facebook. I was absolutely moved
by her courage. Her willingness to "be" in that moment especially moved me. Where I might have allowed pain to drive

me inward to avoid others' emotions, she was authentically vulnerable. My favorite line from her post was, "But when I can, I want to choose life and meaning." What powerful and encouraging words from someone who in her very own words said, "But I will never feel pure joy again." Although I believe she will find joy again, albeit may be different than what she experienced with her husband, I found it refreshing that she shared her true emotions with the world. She chose to connect with the honesty of her feelings, and then gave herself permission to sit with them.

The principle of allowing yourself *to be* is a great accompaniment to the previous principle of allowing yourself to feel. At the most basic level, allowing yourself *to be* provides you with the opportunity to seize the day authentically as the person you were designed and purposed *to be*. We live in an age where external noise tells us who we should be, how we should feel, what we should wear, what car we should purchase, and what school our children should attend. At times it can be hard to listen to everyone and then follow our own internal voice.

A unique strength comes from living life on your own terms. We all need to know that we can be whatever and however we want to be. What happens when you become inundated with work and are juggling too much? From time to time, I get caught up in the craziness of life. When this happens, I've noticed that I'm not connected to my spirit as much as I want to be. I'm often less reflective and not nearly as good at being gentle with myself.

When you feel the need to be anything other than what your spirit demands, the outcome is a drained-and-exhausted you who is disconnected from your purpose, passions, and your source. My favorite thing about recognizing my own inner need *to be* is knowing in that moment I've chosen me over pleasing others, closing my heart, and feeling the ultimate disconnect.

When you feel the need to be anything other than what your spirit demands, the outcome is a drained-and-exhausted you who is disconnected from your purpose, passions, and your source.

Allow Yourself to Be

- Contemplate the barriers that prevent you from being authentic in the moments that matter the most, like a painful loss, life transition, or starting something new.

- Commit to saying exactly what you want to say and to being wholly authentic the next time you feel compelled to go inward or shut down.

- Have a day of "Be" once a quarter. On your of day of "Be," ignore the demands on your time and attention (this might mean disconnecting from electronics and taking the day from work). Do something for yourself that is stimulating and brings you ultimate joy. Connect you to your inner you, and rest there.

REFLECTIONS ON HOW I WILL
Allow Myself to Be

CHAPTER 10
Live for Yourself

*Sometimes you have to do what's best for you and your life,
not what's best for everybody else.*
—Unknown

Most people disassociate with the phrase, "live for yourself." If you're a parent, you might think it's your responsibility to live for your children. On the flip side, as we age, we often weigh the idea of following our dreams against the responsibility placed on us from our parents or community at large. Choosing to live for yourself is often associated with being selfish. I disagree. Living for yourself is the only way to live authentically.

One of my favorite movies is *Runaway Bride* starring Julia Roberts and Richard Gere. In the movie, Julia Roberts's character, Maggie Carpenter, is so plagued with cold feet on her wedding day that she jilts her grooms—leaving a total of five men waiting at the altar. However, in the beginning of each of her relationships, Maggie is so committed to pleasing each of her husbands to-be and becoming "the perfect wife" that she eats her eggs only the way her partners prefer them. This one detail in this movie is amusing because I've met countless people, primarily women, who are like Julia's character. In fact, I too have been like Maggie from time to time. Of course, your life is yours to live. It's a gift, and no one else has the pleasure of being you—someone designed with a particular set of gifts, talents, skills, and preferences. Yet a major barrier to seizing life is the inability to connect with what we truly want for our lives. The small things we give up, like our preference for eggs at breakfast, can lead to compromising on the larger things, like our dream career, ideal city or town, whether or not to have children, or what feeds us spiritually.

> A major barrier to seizing life is our inability to connect with what we truly want for our lives.

How often do you seek to please others or overaccommodate your partners, family members, children, and colleagues?

In an interview with Alyssa DeRusha for my blog, *Carpe Diem with Jasmine*, Alyssa shared why she chose to launch a fashion blog, *Alyssa Styled*. She's the wife of a well-known television news anchor in the Twin Cities, Jason DeRusha, and the mother of two tween-age boys, and she holds a high-pressure job in the financial industry. However, Alyssa launched her blog as a way to explore her passion for all things fashion, and also launched it as something *for her*. Alyssa said that she knows from personal experience how "easy it is to get stuck in a comfort zone," so she decided to live for herself by doing something she never thought she'd do.

I'm always reminded when I fly of how important taking care of and living for one's self is. Every airline's safety demonstration clearly states, "Put on your own oxygen mask before helping those around you." If you don't value yourself, how can you really value and appreciate anything else? Sometimes living for you involves saying no, telling people what they don't want to hear, and implementing healthy boundaries. It's extremely hard for most individuals to purposely put themselves first, and yet it's impossible to seize your life without doing so. Living for yourself can be as simple as adding you to your to-do list, pursuing a personal hobby, or starting your own blog like Alyssa did.

The key is *to remember you*. Your life is yours.

- Choose to be in alignment with who you are at the deepest level.
- Decide to choose to do the things that connect with you at your core.
- Be who you were you designed and destined to be.
- Live by the manifesto that you design, and you'll manifest unimaginable possibilities.
- Tap into your creativity and personal inner power, and you'll connect with the greatest force there is on earth.

Most individuals find it
extremely hard to purposely
put themselves first, and yet
it's impossible to seize your life
without doing so.

CARPE DIEM GUIDELINES TO

Live for Yourself

- Develop a meditation practice by first becoming comfortable with your thoughts.

- Develop a gratitude practice through journaling, daily reflection, or prayer.

- Capture thoughts about 1) the life you want, 2) the experiences you desire to have, and 3) the person you hope to evolve into in a method of your choice.

REFLECTIONS ON HOW I WILL
Live For Myself

CHAPTER 11
Allow Yourself to Dream

Here's to the crazy ones, the misfits, the rebels, the troublemakers, the round pegs in the square holes . . . the ones who see things differently—they're not fond of rules . . . You can quote them, disagree with them, glorify or vilify them, but the only thing you can't do is ignore them, because they change things . . . they push the human race forward, and while some may see them as the crazy ones, we see genius, because the ones who are crazy enough to think that they can change the world are the ones who do.
—*Steve Jobs*

I love hearing stories about people who dare to dream big and then make those dreams come true. Experiencing a dream come true is one of my favorite ways to Carpe Diem. But, while I connect with my dreams every day, I also relish in opportunities to celebrate other people's dreams coming true. As

I watch a dream bloom into reality, I believe even more that dreams aren't meant to *stay* dreams. The power isn't simply in having a dream; it's in knowing that your dreams are possible and then creating a space for them to bloom.

Jacqui and I met more than a year ago at a dinner party while I was visiting the West Coast. Jacqui brought samples of her new Avila called Revel (think tequila but from a different region of Mexico, the way champagne comes from France, and sparkling wine is the bubbly wine made in California) with her to the dinner party. Everyone at the dinner raved about how smooth the Revel tasted. At the time I was taking a brief hiatus from drinking alcohol. Jacqui noted my disappointment, and at the end of my visit to California, she surprised me with a package of Revel samples to take home with me. What a treat. Everyone who raved about it was right. Revel was stellar. I immediately wanted to know how Jacqui, a former music executive who had worked with music icons like Chaka Khan, Carlos Santana, and Prince, was suddenly on this new journey.

After witnessing significant changes in the music industry, Jacqui decided to take her future into her own hands and began to think about her next professional chapter. She asked herself three vital questions: 1) Am I learning? 2) Am I having fun? and 3) Am I making enough money that if the answers to questions one and two are "no," I'd want to stay? She always asked herself these questions as she advanced from one job to the next. In this case, the answer to all three of her questions was a resounding "no," and Jacqui decided it was indeed time for a career change. She had always secretly dreamed of creating a product and, in her previous career, especially enjoyed marketing and merchandising. Through a combination of networking, pursuing opportunities, and leveraging her marketing expertise, she and two friends launched Revel Spirits. Jacqui believes that she and her business partners' networks of advisers, paired with their ability to step out of their comfort zones, led to her dream becoming a reality. Jacqui's story is especially powerful because it proves that it's never too late to begin a new chapter.

> It's never too late to ask yourself if you're truly where you want to be.

What are your dreams? Really. Are you living a dream right now? Dreams are not always an easy investment, because there's that pesky risk that they might not come true. And yet, without them, our life's possibilities become significantly narrower. Daring to dream, and having your dreams come true, means stepping out of your comfort zone, which might mean that you have to get creative. For instance, the founders of Airbnb sold their own brand of cereal to raise capital. Ben Silberman, one of the cofounders of Pinterest, personally wrote to the first 7,000 people who joined to ask for feedback, which he credits as the source for making Pinterest better.

Your dreams might not happen on your timing, and they might not be executed perfectly, but that doesn't matter. Create space for them anyway.

Dreams thrive on resilience. And when you're told "no," or things don't work out, don't sweat it. When you seize a dream and push it toward fruition, you've given yourself a precious gift, whether or not it becomes what you expected.

CARPE DIEM GUIDELINES TO

Allow Yourself to Dream

- Don't be afraid to dream and to dream big, loud, and unapologetically.

- Remember: it's never too late to make a dream come true.

- The dreams you have while sleeping are often trying to tell you something. Pay attention, and when it doubt, write it down.

REFLECTIONS ON HOW I WILL
Allow Myself to Dream

CHAPTER 12
Make Peace with Uncertainty

*No one knows what tomorrow will bring or if we will
be here to see it. The reality of now trumps the promise of
tomorrow, so enjoy the moment for what it is.*
—Frederick A. Babb

Uncertainty is hard. Not knowing what happens next is extremely difficult for most people, including me. We're all wired to want to know what's next—and not only in our lives. Thanks to Facebook, we're consumed with what's going to happen in our friends' lives, too. It's not a coincidence that book and movie sequels are a billion-dollar industry. We love cliffhangers so that we can fixate on the "happily ever after" to come. Whoever invents a working crystal ball will certainly become a bazillionaire.

In March of 2012, I was forced, and not on my own terms, into becoming comfortable with uncertainty. My previous employer announced a 10 percent reduction in headquarters's employees due to "corporate restructuring." In the days and weeks leading up to the day we were to find out if our jobs had been affected, most of my coworkers were understandably stressed. Oddly, I wasn't. The day before the layoffs were to be announced, I had watched an interview with rapper 50 Cent, and I was riveted by something he said. On the topic of worry, he declared, "You can pray or you can worry, but you can't do both, because God will wonder why you're bothering Him." His comment struck a nerve, and that night I prayed for God's will to be done. I didn't worry about getting laid off. Instead, I became comfortable with the uncertainty ahead. In the end, I was laid off, but I knew I would be okay.

I remember writing the following post on my original blog, *Thoughts From Jasmine:*

> I haven't posted a thought from Jasmine in a very long time. It's been on my "to-do list" for days, weeks, and months, yet I never find the time to post. That's changing today.
>
> My life took a big change on June 18, 2012, when I was informed that I was being "displaced" by my employer during the past eight years. Truth be told, it was beyond time for me to go, and the "displacement" I experienced was the forced motivation I needed to get moving.
>
> Moving to what? That's the million-dollar question.

I've always been one of those people who appeared to be a "free spirit." In reality, I'm a very calculated and intentioned person. I don't make a move unless I have a pretty clear understanding of what the outcome is going to be and I'm able to see the entire picture. Since I'm being honest, that's probably why I overstayed my time there. I knew I needed to move on, and I wanted to move on, yet I was scared because I couldn't see the full picture.

So this is a new walk for me—a walk in *uncertainty*, a walk in *trust*, and a walk in *faith*. I'm not sure what exactly the outcome will be. I still have my "list" of things to do, places to go, people to meet, experiences to experience, and I know without a doubt I'll scratch off all the things on my list. Ask me where I'm going to be living six months from now, and I couldn't answer, and probably for the first time in my life, I'm okay with the uncertainty.

My mom gave me a scripture to stand on, and it's been my guiding principle during this walk of uncertainty, trust, and faith:

> *Trust in the Lord with all your heart and lean not on your own understanding; in all your ways submit to him, and he will make your paths straight* (Proverbs 3:5-6).

Making peace with uncertainty means knowing that your fear of uncertainty is okay.

In the years following my 2012 blog post, I have become more comfortable with uncertainty. Cinderella experienced uncertainty, but she didn't allow it to prevent her from enjoying and relishing in the majesty and splendor of the ball. She laughed, danced, and allowed herself to fall in love.

It's inevitable you'll have times of uncertainty in your life. Making peace with uncertainty means knowing that your fear of uncertainty is okay. But don't let fear drive your actions. Don't allow it to prevent you from being open to seizing all that the next chapter has in store for you.

Make Peace with Uncertainty

- Contemplate the reasons you're most afraid of uncertainty. When you journal your thoughts, pay attention to the cues about where you find yourself feeling afraid.

- Make a mental list of those you admire who have thrived, found strength in, or prospered in a season of uncertainty. How did they do it? What can you learn from them?

- Look forward to the next moment when you might experience a feeling of uncertainty. Prepare yourself for the adventure in advance by deciding to embrace the lessons you'll learn and surprises you could not have anticipated.

Make Peace with Uncertainty

CHAPTER 13
Walk in the Spirit of Abundance

Today, expect something good to happen to you no matter what occurred yesterday.
—*Sara Ban Breanthnach*

Most people think only of financial wealth or of accumulating things when they think of the word abundance. But that isn't what I mean when I talk about *abundance*. For our purposes, I'm referring to the spiritual definition: *peace found through feeling that there is enough in the world for everyone to have the desires of their hearts.* When you walk in the spirit of abundance, you create space for infinite possibilities, unexpected opportunities, love, blessings, joy, peace, and grace—all of which transform your everyday moments. Abundance is fuel for your dreams and hopes. Once you believe that you were created for abundance, nothing will stop you from greeting each day with an intention to get the most it has to offer.

> Spiritual definition of abundance: peace found through feeling that there is enough in the world for everyone to have the desires of their hearts.

It's human nature to view things from a perspective that promotes scarcity, competition, and fear. But walking in the spirit of abundance creates a life-changing shift. Abundance says that there is and will always be enough for everyone. For instance, you don't have to begrudge a coworker being promoted or ever wonder when your next break will come. A spirit of abundance assumes that life will lead you where you belong and that your desires are not only possible but also inescapable. It infuses your mindset with expectation for extraordinary things to happen to you no matter your circumstances or surroundings.

> A spirit of abundance assumes
> that life will lead you where you
> belong and that your desires are
> not only possible, but inescapable.

For me, no one embodies walking in the spirit of abundance more than Malala Yousafzai. Malala is a vigilant activist for female education and human rights in her native Pakistan. She is also the youngest recipient of the Nobel Peace Prize. Malala's father, also an education activist, says he always knew his daughter was special. At a young age, Malala determined that education was her right, despite the fact the Taliban, who governed her war-torn region, forbid women to be educated. After an assassination attempt on her life, Malala became a beacon of hope for women across the world. She's changed the world through her work against the suppression of children and young people. Malala refused to believe that progress and education were beyond her reach. She chose to believe that her dreams and purpose would be realized in abundance.

When you choose to walk in the spirit of abundance, you are able to take action without giving into pressure, fear, and self-doubt, even if costs you. I love what author Sara Ban Breanthnach wrote in her *New York Times* bestselling book, *Simple Abundance*: "The revelation that we have everything we need

in life to make us happy but simply lack the conscious awareness to appreciate it can be as refreshing as lemonade on a hot
afternoon. Or it can be as startling as cold water being thrown
in our face. How many of us go through our days parched and
empty, thirsting after happiness, when we're really standing
knee-deep in the river of abundance?"

Walk in the Spirit of Abundance

• Think about what your definition of abundance is. What would it mean to know that your wishes, desires, and hopes *will* be realized?

• Write down your deepest dream.

• Reflect from a space of gratitude on the areas in your life that embody abundance.

Walk in the Spirit of Abundance

CHAPTER 14
Practice Gratitude

"Piglet noticed that even though he had a Very Small Heart, it could hold a rather large amount of Gratitude."
—*A.A. Milne,* Winnie-the-Pooh

People often ask how to begin to Carpe Diem or "seize the day." For me, the answer is simple: gratitude. When you move in gratitude with the realization of what you have to be thankful for, you'll start to notice a change in your life almost immediately. In today's oversensationalized society focused on headline and sound bites, it's easy to reside in a state of doom and gloom. Practicing gratitude shifts the energy and allows us to focus on the good in our lives, families, and communities.

> When you move in gratitude
> with the realization of what
> you have to be thankful for,
> you'll start to notice a change
> in your life almost immediately.

When a relationship ended in my early twenties, I was brokenhearted and in an unshakeable funk. During that period, I returned to writing in my Gratitude Journal to remind me of the many things I had to be thankful for, despite my current state. I started by capturing five things to be thankful for each day. Some days, the list was simple:

1. I'm thankful that I can blink my eyes.
2. I'm thankful to be fully functioning.
3. I'm thankful that I woke up today.
4. I'm thankful that I can walk.
5. I'm thankful to have food to eat.

And some days the list went on and on. Shortly after I began to consistently keep my Gratitude Journal, I experienced an about-face, and all of a sudden it wasn't a S-T-R-E-T-C-H for me to think of five things to be thankful for in a day. It appeared that things were working with and for me instead of against me, and, most importantly, I got my mojo back.

I've learned that you have to be thankful for what the Universe has blessed you with. One of my mom's favorite saying is, "I may not be where I want to be, but I'm thankful for not being where I used to be." Keeping a Gratitude Journal has also been my personal benchmarking tool; it's a visual reference of where I once was and where I am. It's a record of my blessings, prayers, and happenstances—all the splendor of life's gifts that are the foundation of Carpe Diem.

Years later, I still keep a Gratitude Journal. A recent Carpe Diem moment occurred after a really intense week of travel. As I burst through the door, luggage and crankiness in tow, a wonderfully sweet aroma greeted me. I instantly thought, "My plugins are really working!" Then I walked into my living room. My dehydrated jasmine plant was in full bloom on an end table. I had forgotten all about the plant, but it apparently had not forgotten me. What a gift. It showed me that we are presented with opportunities to be grateful every day.

> It's amazing the things you notice and feel when you're not simply going through the motions, or what some refer to as operating in the conscious realm.

I contend that practicing and moving with gratitude is an extension of mindfulness. I believe that when we are truly present, we have the ability to see and receive blessings in abundance. It's like riding in the passenger seat on a route you've traveled one hundred times. Suddenly, as a passenger you notice billboards and the shapes and colors of trees; you see the beauty that has always been there. I now know that focusing on gratitude, and being thankful for what I have and for the beauty surrounding me, is far healthier, not to mention more productive, than allowing fear, anxiety, doubt, worry, or fatigue to overcome me. Without a doubt, no matter what happens, including during the darkest moments, there's always something to be thankful for every day.

Practice Gratitude

- Learn to "practice gratitude," and you'll become more aware of the beauty in your life.

- Make writing in your Gratitude Journal a priority for every day, even when it is hard to find something to be grateful for that day.

- Start your Gratitude Journal by capturing five things, people, events, or occurrences you are thankful for each day.

REFLECTIONS ON HOW I WILL
Practice Gratitude

CHAPTER 15
Use Your Words Carefully

You can change your world by changing your words . . .
Remember, death and life are in the power of the tongue.
—*Joel Osteen*

As a child, when I was picked on or spoken to meanly, my mom and dad would always remind me of the age-old adage, "Sticks and stones may break your bones, but words will never hurt you." Those words were an L-I-E! Words can hurt, but on the other hand, words can be *inspiring, motivating, encouraging,* and *loving.* In his book *The Five Love Languages,* Gary Chapman says words can affirm another person. Who doesn't want to be affirmed or have his or her actions, hopes, and dreams acknowledged, validated, and accepted?

Two different sets of people wrote me touching emails on the same day a few years ago—a married couple, and a mother and daughter—whom I randomly met while out and about in my everyday life. They said they were following up on connecting for the dinner or coffee we had discussed, but they also took the time to tell me how much they enjoyed our conversation and meeting me. Those words really made my day because it was such a pleasant and unexpected compliment.

On the other hand, some words can leave a lingering sting, crush a budding dream, or maybe create havoc. Hearing parents calling their children mean and cruel words like *stupid, bad, dumb,* or *ugly* always saddens and burdens me. I firmly believe that life and death are in the power of the tongue, and while some people have been able to use the negative words said against them as motivation and inspiration to succeed—and also to show the person who spoke those terrible words that he or she was wrong—most people *do not have that ability.*

As one who has been hurt by words said in the heat of the moment, I always try to use my words carefully. Unfortunately, apologies aren't able to erase the scars often left from the wounds created by words. Using your words carefully involves: 1) not always saying the first thing that comes to mind; 2) walking away in a heated argument; 3) taking a moment to pause before speaking; and 4) sometimes allowing the other person to feel he or she is right, even when that person is wrong.

Always use your words carefully.

CARPE DIEM GUIDELINES TO
Use Your Words Carefully

- Take the time to send a card or letter using good, old-fashioned snail mail, writing to your significant other, a friend, or relative letting them know you appreciate them.

- Next time you're in a heated conversation or argument, take a moment to pause or remove yourself from the situation. It would be awful to say something you can't take back.

- Practice speaking positive and encouraging words about stressful and uncomfortable situations and/or people.

Use My Words
Carefully

CHAPTER 16
Have Courage

All that is ever required is for you to just have the courage to be you, and I mean ALL of you.
—Panache Desai

Not too long ago, I received a text from one of my dearest friends, Rachel.

> *Hi! Big news! I mean lots of it! I met a lovely man in South Africa. I went to visit him in the Bahamas where he works on a boat and now I am doing a 2-week crossing with him to France and I leave Monday!*

After reading it, I couldn't text my barrage of questions fast enough. My smartphone keypad screeched, "What? A man. A boat. A two-week crossing of the Atlantic Ocean, and France?" Her news required an immediate phone call, prompting me to break my "no calls before eight a.m." rule to get the full story.

From the text, you might think Rachel is a free spirit, an adventurist who throws caution to wind in pursuit of discovery. What other kind of person agrees to sail across the ocean on a boat for two weeks to dock in Cannes, France, with a man he or she met only a month ago? Later I learned it was actually a yacht. However, if you knew Rachel, you'd know that her voyage to France was, in reality, an enormous leap of faith. She was being courageous. She opened herself to possibilities, overcoming deep-rooted fear as she mustered all of her courage for this adventure.

Years earlier, Rachel and I had been roommates in Antibes, France, the city with the largest yacht marina on the Côte d'Azur. There Rachel met and fell in love with a wonderful man—let's call him Joe—who worked on boats. They fell hard for each other so quickly that she decided to stay in Antibes and also work on boats. Eventually they married, sailed, traveled the world, bought a beautiful home, and were living a loving and fulfilled life together. Everything was picture-perfect.

Sadly, after being together for seven years, Joe died in a tragic boat accident. Rachel's life came to a crashing halt, and for years she lived what felt to me like a pseudo-purgatory—a muddle of grief, disappointment, hurt, and confusion—while she tried to rebuild her life without the wonderful man with whom she had shared her dreams, love, plans, and hope for the future. It was a long and arduous journey to find her way back, not only to love, but also to a full and joyful life.

Rachel found the courage to open her heart after having it crushed; imagine how fear could have prevented her from finding love again—and on a boat of all places. After her tragic experience of losing Joe, many people would have vowed to stay away from boats for eternity, and especially men on boats. No one would have blamed her had she chosen to run the opposite direction.

Soon after receiving that text from Rachel, I stumbled upon a TEDx presentation, "Make Your Own Runway Define You" by Patrice (Afrobella) Grell Yorsik, in which she eloquently states, "Courage leads to opportunity." I believe this wholeheartedly. In my friend's case, her courageous leap lead to a new romantic adventure.

> It takes courage to seize your life, and you can do it in baby steps each day.

WHAT ARE *YOUR* BABY STEPS?

- Where in your life do you need to have courage?
- Do you know where you are most afraid, and how is your fear holding you back?
- Have you avoided a necessary conversation?
- Have you allowed a bad habit to control your life?
- Do you simply need to break through something that's holding you back?

It takes being courageous with small things to find the courage for the bigger things. And remember: without courage, you're merely standing still. What often stands between unlocking courage and releasing fear is our refusal to let go. It's impossible to have one foot in the realm of new possibilities while one foot is still rooted in the stale and stagnant grip of the past. When you can't see the forest for the trees and it feels impossible to take a step forward, ask yourself a simple question: Is my fear of the worse-case scenario worth me remaining stuck?

As Pope Francis recently declared to a virtual audience in the United States, "Be courageous. Move forward." Courage is a virtue that must practiced.

> Without courage, you're merely standing still. Courage means freeing yourself of past regrets and mistakes and taking the necessary steps to move forward

CARPE DIEM GUIDELINES TO
Have Courage

- Write down the areas of your life where you should be more courageous (i.e., speaking up more at work, traveling to a new destination with or without a companion, or ending a toxic relationship).

- Reflect on the last time you did something courageous. What opportunities did it create?

- The next time your intuition prompts you to have courage, ask yourself, "What happens if I'm not courageous in this moment? Am I willing to face the consequence of not having courage in this moment?"

REFLECTIONS ON HOW I WILL

Have Courage

CHAPTER 17
Be a Blessing to Someone Else

The greatest blessing in the whole world is being a blessing.
—Jack Hyles

Recently I was thinking about a friend who has been a true blessing in my life. Shortly afterwards, I opened a fortune cookie that read: *By helping someone today, you may also be helping yourself.* I believe that when we positively impact the lives of others, we inadvertently positively impact our own lives. It's also important to remember that we all have something to give.

> When we positively impact the lives of others, we inadvertently positively impact our own lives.

One of my mom's employees, Ms. Prince, has the kindest spirit, and she's an *amazing* cook. Not a foodie cook or a gourmet, but a good ol' Southern cook making food the way the grandmas and big mommas of the old South use to prepare food. She works at a school where the majority of students receive free and reduced-cost lunch, or what is often referred to as a Title I school. She's also the matriarch of her family and takes care of her ill daughter and grandchildren. However, she still finds a way to prepare dinner for her students and their parents every Friday. Ms. Prince is not able to solve the majority of the problems and issues the students and families at her school cope with, but she's able to be a blessing to members of the community by sharing her gift of cooking. Due to work schedules, timing, ability, and resources, they seldom have the opportunity to get a fresh, home-cooked meal that didn't come out of a box or from the freezer.

For whatever reason, I smile ninety percent of the time. It used to bother me when someone would ask me why I smile all the time. Can't a person have a happy disposition? Now, I simply reply, "Would you prefer me to frown?" All kidding aside, I've realized that people aren't used to seeing strangers smile. At times I may not have much to physically offer others, but a smile is a blessing I can always share.

> A smile is a blessing
> you can always share
> with others.

Here's a challenge: intentionally help someone this week. It could be as simple as offering to assist someone with carrying a heavy load, buying groceries for someone you know who has lost her job, or calling your grandmother simply to chat. Be that unexpected *blessing* for someone this week, and see how your life will be *blessed in return.*

Have you ever thought about how much it costs to say, "Hello," the energy you exert when smiling, or how much time it takes to sincerely ask someone how he or she is doing, listen to his answer, and reply accordingly?

> You never know how you may bless
> someone by simply asking him how he
> is doing and listening to his reply.

The simple fact that we are able to help someone or provide some type of value gives credence to the idea that we are already *blessed*. Share your blessings by being an unexpected blessing for someone by using whatever you have to offer to the world.

CARPE DIEM GUIDELINES TO

Be a Blessing to Someone Else

- Remember that actions speak louder than words.

- Take the time to get to know a neighbor or coworker over a meal, cup of coffee, or glass of wine. You'll be surprised by what you are able to learn about a person by listening to him or her.

- Speak words of kindness, encouragement, and acceptance to those around you.

Be a Blessing to Someone Else

CHAPTER 18
Time Waits for No One, and You Shouldn't Either— Do it Now

Don't wait for extraordinary opportunities.
Seize common occasions and make them great.
Weak men wait for opportunities; strong men make them.
—Orison Sett Marden

One morning, I watched "CBS This Morning" while on the treadmill. I saw a story about Justice Clarence Thomas making history by breaking his streak of seven years of silence on the bench. The story went on to explain that the other Supreme Court Justices can be very abrasive towards lawyers presenting arguments and make disrespectful comments to the presenting attorneys. I thought . . . *wow*, how cool would it be to see a case argued in the Supreme Court live and in person. Maybe I'll take a day off from work sometime this year and observe the arguments at the Supreme Court. Then I thought, Jasmine, you went to college in Washington, DC; you could have easily spent a day, two days, or a week at the Supreme Court. *A missed opportunity.*

I had the opportunity to attend the 57th Presidential Inauguration in 2013—President Barack Obama's second inauguration. Standing immediately over to the left of the row I was sitting in was Paula Abdul. A bunch of people took pictures of her, and a few people actually walked over to take a picture with her. I wanted to also, but thought I should be respectful of her personal time and allow her to enjoy her time at the inauguration. Later that evening, I sent her a tweet and she replied that she would've *loved* to meet me and take a picture. *A missed opportunity.*

The evening, when I returned home from the week in Washington, D.C., I received a phone call from my friend Erica asking me to call her back that night no matter what time I picked up her voicemail. When I called her around 11:30 p.m., she shared her bad news: her mother had lost her battle to cancer and passed away on Monday. Shock ran through my body. I knew her mom had been ill, but I didn't know she was *that* ill. Now I remembered that Erica called me the week before, but her voicemail said she was calling to catch up. Since I had no major new developments to report, and due to my "busyness," I had not returned her call. *A missed opportunity.*

I've had my share of missed opportunities, and I recognize that it's impossible to do everything, but my challenge to myself and to you is to make sure you are doing the *right* things and the *important* things. Don't allow those things to become missed opportunities due to busyness, fear, laziness, complacency, the weather, not having your hair done, not having anything to wear, etc., because you never know if you'll get another opportunity.

Don't allow those things to become missed opportunities because you never know if you'll get another opportunity.

CARPE DIEM GUIDELINES TO
Do It Now

- Reflect on your missed opportunities, and why you missed them.

- When planning and scheduling, leave some time open for unplanned opportunities and experiences.

- Release limiting beliefs like: you aren't worthy, qualified or deserving of an opportunity.

REFLECTIONS ON HOW I WILL
Do It Now

CHAPTER 19
Be Still, Listen, and Know

"Be still, and know that I am God"
—Psalms 46:10

We live in an extremely fast-paced society. I can count the times this year that I have been able to complete everything on my daily "to-do list." E-mail is an always-available communication tool, and people often expect a response in less than twenty-four hours. We no longer have—or take—the time to engage in telephone conversations, so we send short messages made up of acronyms like SYS, OMW, TTYL, or HYD to convey the messages we need to communicate. Due to the fast pace at which change can occur, we often find ourselves managing through ambiguity in our personal and professional lives because no one has time, we make things up on the fly, and we recalculate and adjust as needed. We very seldom, if ever, take time to be still, listen, and know.

Recently, several well-known and respected business leaders have said that they practice meditation because it gives them an edge in the competitive business world. These include: Arianna Huffington, President & Editor-in-Chief of Huffington Post Media Group; Bill Ford, Executive Chairman of Ford Motor Company; Tony Schwartz, Founder & CEO of The Energy Project; Marc Benioff, CEO of Salesforce; Ray Dalio, Founder & CEO of Bridgewater Associates; and Oprah Winfrey, CEO & Chief Creative Officer of OWN, The Oprah Winfrey Network; Oprah.com; O, The Oprah Magazine; and Harpo Films. At its basic level, meditation is the slowing down, silencing, and stopping of the ongoing chatter, thoughts, and activities that race through our minds daily like Olympic sprinters training for the gold.

> Meditation is the slowing down, silencing, and stopping of the ongoing chatter, thoughts, and activities that race through our minds daily.

These leaders recognize that the mind must be given time to rest and be still. The stillness found in meditative practices, or by taking the time to be still, provides an opportunity for us to listen to our inner voice and to God. We live in a time when we are constantly receiving information, and our senses are overloaded with various things: noise from the sound of typing on computer keys, earbuds playing our favorite playlist from Spotify, the perfume the person in the next cubicle is wearing, or homemade lunch seeping out of its container. I recently read in *The Art of Stillness* by Pico Iyer that the amount of information that the average American takes in during a single day is equivalent to what Shakespeare took in during his entire life. When do we have time to be still and listen to our inner voice or to God?

I have to take the time to be still, to listen, and to know that all will be well in order to seize the day. I do that through prayer, meditation, and long bubble baths by candlelight and by not bringing a cellphone, tablet, or laptop into bed with me at night. In fact, I leave my smartphone in the kitchen at night to allow my brain to stop. Before I did this, if I woke in the middle of the night, I'd grab my smartphone to read emails or check out Facebook until I was able to fall back asleep.

When do we have time to be still and listen to our inner voice or to God?

Kevin Kelly, Founding Executive Editor of *Wired* Magazine, frequently takes long trips through Asian villages to allow himself to be "rooted in the nonvirtual world," according to Pico Iyer. Kevin's ritual of traveling as a way of disconnecting with the virtual world is a reminder for all of us that we have to take the time to be still, to listen, and to know—because it's the only way we will remember who we are.

"May today there be peace within. May you trust God that you are exactly where you are meant to be. May you not forget the infinite possibilities that are born of faith. May you use those gifts that you have received and pass on the love that has been given to you. May you be content knowing you are a child of God. Let this presence settle into your bones, and allow your soul the freedom to sing, dance, praise, and love. It is there for each and every one of us."
—*St. Teresa of Avila*

Be Still, Listen, and Know

- Take a technology day off. Shut down your computer, turn off your cell phone, unplug your tablet, and click off the television for an entire day.

- Dedicate at least five minutes a day to sitting still in silence.

- Work to develop your own daily prayer or meditation practice that works well in your lifestyle, and provides you with an opportunity to be still, listen, and know.

REFLECTIONS ON HOW I WILL

Be Still, Listen, and Know

CHAPTER 20
Change Your Perspective

"Life is 10 percent what you make it and
90 percent how you take it."
—Irving Berlin

One morning I woke up with the word "perspective" top of mind. When I think about perspective, I envision two people standing in a museum looking at the same picture. One person sees a terrible thunderstorm, and the other person sees people dancing in the rain.

How can that be? Aren't the two people looking at the *same picture?*

I contend that they see the painting differently because they are looking at it with different internal lenses, which provide their perspective. For many people, perspective is based on external factors that alter their internal lenses—comfort level, community, politics, family, friends, work environment, the weather, and sometimes, the alignment of the moon and stars can all affect one's perspective.

Yes, I live in Minneapolis, and really do enjoy living there—April through October. Ask me how life is in Minneapolis around January 14th, and I'll tell you I'm ready to pack my things and move back South. How can that be, when three months ago I was in love with the city? Old Man Winter has showed up and changed my perspective.

Have you ever been in a rut? Doing the same thing, with the same people, telling and laughing at the same jokes day after day. In that case, a little trip somewhere different, a conversation with an old college friend, or a visit to a local nursing home could provide a much-needed change of perspective to get you out of your rut.

Yes, our lives are like mosaics. Our experiences of the good, bad, ugly, and indifferent are the pieces of broken tile that come together to make something beautiful. I will embrace all my wounds and scars, but I'm not going to allow them to taint my perspective.

Sometimes seizing the day could be as easy as changing your perspective about a person or situation.

Change Your Perspective

- Mentally play devil's advocate. Take a position that you don't necessarily agree with on an issue or situation.

- Do something out of your comfort zone. For example, visit a church with a congregation made of a different race than yours.

- Change your scenery . . . maybe plan a trip, eat at a new restaurant, or go to a grocery store in a different neighborhood.

REFLECTIONS ON HOW I WILL

Change My Perspective

CONCLUSION

Sometimes the best things in life are those that are often misunderstood. I remember when I was younger, and also recently, my mother warning me *not to become common*. She was basically telling me to dare to be different in an "old-school, read-between-the-lines" kind of way. She was encouraging me to go against the grain.

So often we become common as we fall prey to the status quo. We do things because other people are doing them, we fall victim to peer pressure, or we try to keep up with "The Joneses." The status quo is not necessarily a bad thing. In common land, people are often accepted and quite comfortable, but why settle for comfort *when you can be great*?

It's okay to be misunderstood. Look at Albert Einstein, Kanye West, Wendy Williams, and Bill Clinton. Decisions these individuals have made have been misunderstood and scrutinized by the general public, but each person has definitely left a mark on modern-day society.

> Be a little misunderstood.
> It's okay . . . let's settle
> for greatness.

Life is short. No one knows the moment, second, minute, hour, day, month, or year he or she is going to die. You could choke on a chicken bone or go peacefully in your sleep one night. My point: no one is invincible, and as Chris Rock said in his comedic song, "No Sex in the Champagne Room," . . . "you're gonna die."

Knowing I am going to die has made me very intentional about the life I live. My personal mantra is Carpe Diem (seize the day). We have to make it our personal mission to *seize the day*. No one is going to make sure you are happy, that you spent enough time with your family, that you took vacations, or that you went to the doctor for your yearly physical. It is each individual's responsibility to make sure that she is seizing the day because all we really have is *this day*.

> Take some time to
> reflect on the life you are
> living. Are you living each day
> to its fullest?

Americans are obsessed with status, toys, titles, and money, but do those things really add to our lives? They may provide temporary happiness, but they don't define people. When we die, it's not the things that others will miss about us, nor will they be our legacy. It's the lives we have touched that will be impacted the most by our time here on earth.

> *Yesterday's the past, tomorrow's the future, but today is a gift. That's why it's called the present.*
> *—Bill Keane*

ACKNOWLEDGMENTS

My list of thank yous could go on for days, but in the spirit of brevity I would like to extend the most sincerest thank you to every single person who has supported me on this journey to share my thoughts on *Seizing Your Life* and how to *Carpe Diem* with the world through a book. Know that your deeds and names are permanently etched on my heart.

To my mom, thank you for modeling what it means to Carpe Diem every day, way before I knew what Carpe Diem meant. Thank you for your love, support, advice, critiques, encouragement, and always answering my late-night phone calls. More importantly, thank you for truly being the wind beneath my wings.

To my very own 007, thank you for your unwavering and unconditional support, encouragement, and love. I'm *planning* for this book to be a *huge success*.

To my dad, thank you for being the president and founder of the Jasmine Brett Stringer fan club. I appreciate your perspective and confidence in my abilities. I hope I have made you proud.

To my friend, writing consultant and publisher, Dara Irene Beevas at Wise Ink, thank you for the late nights, the questioning and probing, and more importantly, for challenging me to follow my passion—instead of doing what I perceived *as being easier.*

To the team of people that have touched this book at Wise Ink Publishing: Dara Beevas, Patrick Maloney, Amy Quale, Laura Zats; my editor, Connie Anderson; and my cover designer, Nupoor Gordon, THANK YOU for your patience, compassion, and the countless hours you worked to bring this book into existence.

To my dear friend, Kimberley Bow Sundy, thank you for keeping me accountable with your friendly reminders, suggestions, and comments. You've mastered "being subtle." You're the best friend and cheerleader a person could have.

To my friend Erica Corbett, thank you for your friendship, and for all of the work you do behind the scenes on my behalf. I'm so glad you found your graphic artist muse again.

Thank you to my village: Aunt Irma, Aunt Sandy, my "sister" Sandy, Momma Connie, Mr. and Mrs. P, the DIVAs, Aunt Sarah, Cousin Regina, Pam and Emmanuel, Cousin Laverta, Ms. Reatha, Reverend Gloria Roach Thomas, Laverne Knighton, and The Mims for your continuous guidance, reassurance, and love.

To my "framily"—friends who have become family. The adage that you can pick your friends but not your family is no longer true. Thank you for becoming additional members of my family.

To my friend, the beautiful Lisa Sockolov. Thank you for sharing your lovely home with me, and allowing it to become my writing retreat. And also for your steadfast support and encouragement.

To my virtual friend, Jay Grewal, thank you for your timely

messages of support and encouragement. You always seemed to send a message when I needed it most. I appreciate you traveling on this journey with me.

To my publicist, Robyn Stevens, thank you for helping me build my brand and spread my Carpe Diem message. Here's to creating a movement.

To my beta readers, thank you for taking the time to read selected chapters or the entire book, and for providing me with your honest feedback.

Thank you to two of my Riverwood High School English teachers, Ms. Robinson, for introducing me to Horace, and to Mr. Bounds (a.k.a. Coach Bounds) for planting a seed of writing through your countless writing assignments and harsh grading.

Thank you to the *OWN Ambassadors* community for being a like-minded group of friends that provides a safe place for me to be vulnerable.

To my personal angels Tyrone Maycock, Charmaine Marks, Ernestine Lindsey, Johnnie and Edna Robinson, Ernestine Darden, and Rev. Ed Ridgeway. Thank you all for guiding and working with the Universe to conspire on my behalf.

Thank you to everyone who has encouraged me to write by providing a compliment, a comment on a blog post, or by simply reading my blog. A huge thank you to everyone who is supporting this project by reading this book or by purchasing a copy.

To God be the glory for all the things you have done for me. All that I am and ever hope to be I owe it all to Thee.

ABOUT THE AUTHOR

Jasmine Brett Stringer is principal of JB Stringer LLC and founder of the internationally recognized lifestyle brand, *Carpe Diem with Jasmine*. Jasmine is a graduate of American University's Kogod School of Business in Washington, D.C. She was named a *Woman of Promise* by the Girl Scouts in 2012. She was recognized as a Distinguished Alumna of American University, and *Ebony Magazine* featured her as one of their "*30 Future Leaders . . . in America.*"

As a recognized and sought-after lifestyle expert, Jasmine has been featured on a variety of media outlets. She is a lifestyle contributor to local CBS television station WCCO-TV, a regular contributor to the nationally syndicated television show, *The Insider*, and featured on OWN TV. Her Southern-belle charm is not limited to the screen; Jasmine teaches others to seize their life as a regular contributor for the *Huffington Post* and within her own lifestyle blog entitled, *Carpe Diem with Jasmine.*

Oprah Winfrey has called Jasmine a carrier of the light, and Jasmine continually teaches all the mantra of *carpe diem*, or seize the day. She guides people in identifying their goals and achieving their definition of success through workshops and seminars.

Jasmine is available is for speaking, workshops, and

coaching. She can be reached at info@jbstringer.com or www.carpediemwithjasmine.com.